Timberline Lodge Cookbook

Timberline Mt. Hood, Oregon

1937

Sun   M

3   4
10   11   12
17   18   19   23
24   25   26   27   28   29   30
31

Timberline Lodge Cookbook

Timberline Executive Chef
Leif Eric Benson

Food Photographer
Edward Gowans

Writer
Sara Perry

Designer
Judith Ann Rose

Food Stylist
Carolyn Schirmacher Gerould

TM

Graphic Arts Center Publishing Company
Portland, Oregon

Editor-in-Chief
Douglas A. Pfeiffer

Project Director and Designer
Judith Ann Rose

Timberline Lodge Executive Chef
Leif Eric Benson

Food Photographer
Edward Gowans

Stylist
Carolyln Schirmacher Gerould

Writer
Sara Perry

Calligrapher
Inga Dubay

Recipe Editor
Rosemary Barrett

Book Manufacturing
Lincoln & Allen Company

International Standard Book Number 0-932575-86-2
Library of Congress Catalogue Card Number 88-82192

Printed in the United States of America
Third Printing

Acknowledgments

The authors and editor wish to thank the following individuals for their valuable contributions to the production of this book: Barbara Brooks, home economist; Linda Dixon, photographer's assistant; Shelley Bedell-Stiles, proofreader; Valerie Schuyler, index editor; Stephen Gerould, potter; Kelly Orr, designer; Dee Frank, mechanicals; and Linny Adamson, curator of Timberline Lodge.

A special thanks goes to the entire Timberline Lodge culinary team for their committed professionalism. It is their creative energy that is the trademark of Timberline cuisine.

Our thanks to publishers Mike Hopkins and Doug Pfeiffer for their initial confidence and continued support.

We are especially grateful to our good friend, Richard Kohnstamm, operator of Timberline Lodge, for his guidance. We also wish to acknowledge his inspiration for this project and his continued influence upon this extraordinary landmark.

Generous assistance toward
the publication of this book
was provided by Timberline Lodge

Contents

Introduction

Timberline Lodge—the building and its setting—holds a special place in the hearts of Oregonians and travelers from around the world. It stands just above the timberline of Mt. Hood, Oregon's highest peak. Built during the Depression from the mountain's natural resources of timber and stone, the Lodge is a magnificent living monument to the skilled WPA craftsmen and artisans who created what has become one of the finest alpine hotels in the world.

The cuisine of Timberline has been inspired by the timeless beauty of the Lodge, the lush surroundings of the Pacific Northwest, and the wealth of the best, freshest seasonal foods. Fragrant, jewel-like berries, buttery rich hazelnuts, and exquisite, regional wine grapes are grown in the volcanic-rich soils of Oregon's green valleys. Wild and rare chanterelles and morels thrive on the mountainsides. Prized beef is raised in the high desert country of Central Oregon, and the glittering Columbia River salmon and sweet Dungeness crab flourish in the Pacific Northwest rivers and ocean.

In developing this book, I have assembled some of our favorite and most requested recipes. These dishes are organized according to season, using the natural resources of the Pacific Northwest. You will find among these pages regional specialties and time-honored classics. These recipes reflect what I think cooks want today—honest food that is delicious and simple to prepare but has the timeless elements of tradition and creativity. From our kitchen to yours, we hope that you will share the bounty of Oregon and the legacy of Timberline Lodge with others at your table.

Leif Eric Benson
Timberline Executive Chef

Spring

Columbia River Salmon Coulibiac
Brie en Croûte
Cascade Granola
Blue Heron Tiropitas
Crimson Rhubarb Sorbet
Poached Salmon with Raspberry Hollandaise
Newport Steamed Mussels
Rack of Lamb Mendocino
Pommes Astoria
Spring Run Chinook Tartare
Lapin Sauté aux Champignons
Seafood Salad Coos Bay

Columbia River Salmon Coulibiac

*When using frozen **puff pastry**, be sure to defrost it overnight in the refrigerator and keep refrigerated until it is ready to use. When baked, this dough separates and "puffs" into a myriad of delicate pastry layers.*

Serves 4

1 pound fresh salmon fillet, ¾ to 1 inch thick
1 pound fresh spinach, washed, chopped, and cooked
1 hard-boiled egg
¾ cup white fish, such as cod, sole or snapper, cooked
1 medium onion, chopped
1 tablespoon butter
1 cup cooked wild rice
½ cup Béchamel Sauce (see Master Recipe)
1 tablespoon chopped fresh dill (or 2 teaspoons dried)
1 tablespoon thyme
   zest of 1 lemon
   salt and white pepper to taste
1 12-ounce sheet frozen puff pastry, thawed
   egg wash:
      1 egg
      1 tablespoon water
1 cup Hollandaise Sauce (see Master Recipe)

While spring finds Mt. Hood deeply covered with snow, the delicious combination of fresh salmon and spinach in this elegant Polish dish reminds us that the growing season has arrived in Oregon's rivers and farmlands.

Preheat the oven to 350°.
Skin the salmon and remove any bones. Set aside.
Sauté the onion in the butter until translucent.
Combine the spinach, hard-boiled egg, white fish, sautéed onion, wild rice, Béchamel Sauce, dill, thyme, and lemon zest. Mix lightly and season to taste with the salt and pepper. Set aside.
Roll out the puff pastry sheet so that it is twice the length of the salmon fillet plus 2 inches and 1½ to 2 inches wider than the fillet. At this point, the pastry should be about ⅛ inch thick. If it is thicker, continue rolling until it is the proper thickness.
Spread a layer of the spinach mixture in the middle of the pastry. Place the salmon fillet on the spinach and then spread another layer of the spinach mixture over the salmon. Beat together the egg and water. Fold the pastry over the filling and seal it with egg wash. Turn it so that the seam side is down.
Place on a greased cookie sheet and bake at 350° for 30 to 45 minutes, or until brown. The internal temperature of the salmon should be 130° when done. It may be tested with a meat thermometer.
Slice 1 inch thick and serve with Hollandaise Sauce.

Approximate preparation time: 2 hours

Brie en Croûte

This simple and dramatic dish works well for a small gathering or a large party. The Brie can be substituted with any soft cheese that has a rind, such as Camembert, St. André, or Coulommiers.

Serves 6-8

8 ounce wheel of Brie
1 teaspoon fresh thyme
1 teaspoon chopped fresh basil
4 ounces frozen puff pastry, thawed
    egg wash:
        1 egg
        1 tablespoon water

For a recipe that serves a party of 50, follow the same preparation instructions using these quantities:

5½ pounds Brie
 2 tablespoons fresh thyme
 2 tablespoons chopped fresh Basil
30 ounces frozen puff pastry, thawed
    egg wash:
        1 egg
        1 tablespoon water

Preheat oven to 400°.
Roll the puff pastry into two 6-inch squares about ⅛ inch thick.
Place the Brie in the center of one of the squares and sprinkle evenly with the thyme and basil. Combine the egg and water. Brush the edges of the pastry with egg wash and cover with the second sheet of pastry. Press the two sheets of dough together where they meet. Trim the dough to a circle by removing the corners, and seal the edges with a fork. Brush the pastry with egg wash.
Place on a greased cookie sheet and bake at 400° for 10 minutes, or until brown. Allow to cool 20 minutes before cutting into wedges. Serve as an appetizer with sliced French bread or crackers and fruit.

Approximate preparation time: 20 minutes

Located on the northern slope of Mt. Hood, Lost Lake is a favorite fishing and camping area for outdoor enthusiasts. Since motorboats are prohibited, the tranquil beauty of the area remains undisturbed.

Originally made at Timberline as a high-energy snack to be taken on a ski-lift or forest trail, this delicious combination of nuts, grains, fruit, and golden honey has become a favorite and healthy breakfast cereal.

Cascade Granola

    3 cups old-fashioned rolled oats
    ⅓ cup slivered almonds
    ⅓ cup chopped walnuts
    ⅓ cup grated coconut
    ⅓ cup chopped pecans
 4½ teaspoons cinnamon
 2½ teaspoons cloves
 1½ teaspoons nutmeg
    ⅓ cup raisins
    ⅓ cup honey
    ¼ cup peanut oil
 1½ teaspoons vanilla extract
    2 tablespoons dark corn syrup

Yield: 2½ quarts

For a larger batch, follow the same preparation instructions using the following quantities:

24 cups old-fashioned rolled oats
 4 cups slivered almonds
 4 cups chopped walnuts
 4 cups grated coconut
 4 cups chopped pecans
 ½ cup cinnamon
 ¼ cup cloves
 2 tablespoons nutmeg
 4 cups raisins
 4 cups honey
 3 cups peanut oil
 ¼ cup vanilla extract
 1 cup dark corn syrup

Yield: 3 gallons

Preheat the oven to 350°.
Mix all the dry ingredients except the raisins. In a saucepan, combine the honey, oil, vanilla, and corn syrup, and bring to a boil. Mix the hot liquid with the spiced oat-nut mixture. Bake at 350° for 30 minutes, stirring every 5 minutes. Add the raisins and cool. Store in an airtight container.

Approximate preparation time: 1 hour

Blue Heron Tiropitas

This recipe calls for phyllo pastry which can be found in most freezer sections of the grocery store, or where Middle Eastern food is sold. It is not difficult to use this paper-thin dough; the secret is to keep the phyllo moist while working with it. After the layers are separated and brushed with melted butter, they are baked. The result is a delicate, crisp pastry. This appetizer can be converted into a delicious main course by adding chopped, cooked spinach and/or cooked seafood.

Serves 8

Filling:
    1 cup grated Tillamook cheddar cheese
    ½ cup grated Kasseri cheese
    ½ cup crumbled Feta cheese
    4 ounces cream cheese
    ¼ cup minced green onion
1 pound box phyllo pastry
1 cup butter, melted

    garnish with parsley (optional)

Preheat oven to 425°.
Mix filling ingredients well.
    Cut the phyllo pastry into 5 or 6 equal strips by dividing the longer side of the rectangle. Taking one strip of phyllo at a time, brush with melted butter. Place a second strip on top of the first and brush with butter. Continue layering and brushing with butter until there are four layers of phyllo. Place 2 tablespoons of filling near the upper right hand corner of each strip and fold the upper left hand corner over to enclose the filling. Continue folding as a flag would be folded, creating a triangular pastry with the filling completely enclosed. Repeat the process until all pastries are formed. Brush with butter again and bake about 5 minutes at 425°. When the pastries are golden brown, turn them over to brown the other side. Bake another 5 minutes approximately. Serve immediately with parsley garnish.

Approximate preparation time: 30 minutes

Note: These freeze very well.

Crimson Rhubarb Sorbet

Serves 8

1 pound fresh rhubarb, trimmed
1 cup Pinot Noir (or other dry red wine)
1 cup water
1 cup sugar

garnish with fresh mint
champagne (optional)

In preparing this versatile sorbet, use your favorite Oregon Pinot Noir. The grape used in making this wine is considered one of the finest red wine grapes in the world. Oregon's grape growing area is primarily west of the Cascades where mild and rainy weather helps to produce delicate wines that have complexity and depth.

Chop the rhubarb into 1 inch pieces. Place in a 3-quart saucepan and add the wine, water, and sugar. Bring to a boil and simmer for 10 minutes. Remove from heat and let cool. Purée the mixture in a food processor or blender.

Freeze in an ice cream freezer, following the manufacturer's directions. It should take 35 to 45 minutes to set. Serve as a palate cleanser before the entrée or as a dessert garnished with fresh mint. The sorbet may also be served with 1 ounce of champagne poured over each serving. Serve immediately.

Approximate preparation time: 20 minutes to prepare, 45 minutes to freeze

In a moist, shaded area along a Timberline trail, wild columbine welcomes spring hikers. Another spring arrival, fresh salmon is shown here as a fillet with a classic hollandaise sauce and raspberry purée.

Poached Salmon with Raspberry Hollandaise

Serves 6

6 6-ounce portions of salmon fillet
Salmon Fumet:
    4 cups water
  ½–¾ pound salmon scraps
    ¼ cup chopped onion
    ¼ cup chopped carrot
    ¼ cup chopped celery
    1 whole clove
    ⅛ teaspoon thyme
    ½ bay leaf
    1 cup Chardonnay (or other dry white wine)
Hollandaise Sauce (see Master Recipe)
Raspberry Sauce (see Master Recipe)

In a stockpot, bring the fumet ingredients to a boil. Do not stir. Skim the foam off the top. Simmer for 30 minutes and put through a strainer.

Prepare one recipe each of Hollandaise Sauce and Raspberry Sauce.

Poach the salmon fillets in the salmon fumet for approximately 10 minutes, or until just done. Serve topped with Hollandaise. Trickle Raspberry Sauce over top in a decorative pattern.

Approximate preparation time: 1 hour

Note: This dish is excellent served with boiled, small new potatoes.

When choosing fresh fish from the market, make sure its skin is shiny and bright, its gills red, and its odor clean and fresh. Buying portioned fish, enclosed in cellophane, is risky. If you are purchasing a salmon fillet or steak, make sure the meat is firm and resilient.

Newport Steamed Mussels

Serves 6

6 pounds mussels
2 cups water
¾ cup Oregon Chardonnay (or other dry white wine)
2 tablespoons minced shallots
1 tablespoon chopped fresh dill (or 2½ teaspoons dried)
1 tablespoon fresh chopped garlic
2 tablespoons chopped parsley
  juice of 1 lemon
2 tablespoons butter
1 cup diced fresh tomato (about 2 medium tomatoes)

  garnish with ¼ cup minced green onion

Pacific Northwest mussels, known for their tender meat and mild flavor, are becoming a favorite shellfish among Oregonians. This bivalve mollusk is easy to spot, clustered in Oregon tidepools and attached to harbor pilings by its strong filaments, or beards. This recipe is a simple and elegant way to prepare mussels and to retain their fresh sea-flavor.

    Clean the mussels by scrubbing thoroughly and pulling off and discarding the "beard" or filaments.
    Place the mussels in a large pot with the water, white wine, shallots, dill, garlic, parsley, lemon juice, and butter. Cover and bring to a boil until the mussel shells open.
    Remove the mussels and set aside in a warm place. Boiling it rapidly, reduce the cooking liquid by half. Add the tomato and green onion. Pour over the mussels and serve.

Approximate preparation time: 30 minutes

Rack of Lamb Mendocino

A crust of stone-ground mustard seals in the succulent, delicate flavor of Washington's prized Ellensburg Valley lamb.

Serves 4 to 6

Sauce:
  1½ pounds lamb scraps
  1 medium onion, finely chopped
  2 stalks celery, finely chopped
  2 carrots, peeled and finely chopped
  2 quarts water
  salt and pepper to taste
  1 bay leaf
  2 cloves garlic
  ¾ cup Pinot Noir (or other dry red wine)
  ½ cup butter
  ½ cup flour
  salt and pepper to taste
  4 pounds fresh Oregon rack of lamb, trimmed, with the fat cap removed
  kosher salt
  coarsely ground black pepper
  1 tablespoon prepared stone-ground mustard
  ½ cup bread crumbs
  ¼ cup grated Gruyère or Swiss cheese

First prepare the sauce. This dish is prepared most quickly if the sauce is brought up to the point of melting the butter and adding the flour. Then prepare the lamb, finishing the sauce while the lamb cooks.

Preheat the oven to 450° and roast the lamb scraps and vegetables for 30 minutes, or until browned. Put the vegetables, lamb scraps, and seasonings in a saucepan. Add the water and wine, and simmer, or cook at a very gentle boil, until the liquid is reduced by half. Strain the liquid. Skim the fat. Melt the butter over a high heat until the foam subsides. Stir in the flour and cook, stirring constantly for another 3 minutes. Add the previously prepared lamb stock. Boil a few more minutes and season to taste with salt and pepper. Cover and set aside.

Rub the lamb racks with kosher salt and coarse pepper. Broil about 5 minutes, or until browned. (The racks may also be browned in a sauté pan with butter or oil over a high heat.) Coat the browned racks with mustard. Mix the bread crumbs and cheese, and press onto the racks. Place a meat thermometer in the thickest part of the meat. Roast in a 425° oven for 30 minutes, or until the meat thermometer reads 130°. If desired, cut into chops.

Rewarm the sauce if it has cooled. Serve with the sauce on the side.

Approximate preparation time: 2 hours

Pommes Astoria

Serves 6

4 cups diced red potatoes
4 cups Chicken Stock (see Master Recipe or use canned)
1 cup Béchamel Sauce (see Master Recipe)
½ cup hot-smoked salmon
½ cup minced green onion
1 tablespoon fresh dill (or 2 teaspoons dried)
1 teaspoon lemon zest, grated
  salt and pepper to taste

  Boil the diced red potatoes in Chicken Stock about 20 minutes until tender. Do not overcook. Put into a baking dish and chill.
  Preheat the oven to 350°.
  Heat the Béchamel Sauce. Flake the salmon and add it to the sauce with the green onion, dill, and lemon zest. Season with salt and pepper. Simmer the sauce 10 minutes. Pour over the chilled potatoes. Bake at 350° for 30 minutes.

Approximate preparation time: 1 hour

A messenger of spring, the wood trillium blooms in Oregon from early March along the coast through June at the higher elevations of Mt. Hood. Other delights of spring are the small, thin-skinned new potatoes whose delicate flavor and smooth texture are complemented by the smoky, rich flavor of cured Pacific Northwest salmon.

There is no simpler or more elegant way to serve and enjoy a freshly caught salmon than in its natural uncooked state—tartare—with champagne or a chilled glass of Oregon sparkling wine.

Spring Run Chinook Tartare

Serves 6–8

1 pound very fresh Chinook salmon fillet
1½ teaspoons grated fresh horseradish
1 tablespoon capers
  juice of 1 lemon
¼ cup minced onion
2 tablespoons chopped parsley
1 anchovy, minced
½ teaspoon prepared stone-ground mustard
2 teaspoons olive oil
  dash of Tabasco sauce (or other red pepper sauce)
  salt and white pepper to taste

When handling horseradish root, be sure to rinse hands carefully and avoid rubbing your eyes; the oils that give horseradish its peppery flavor can irritate the skin and eyes.

Remove any skin or bones from salmon fillet. Cut into 1 inch cubes. Place the salmon in a food processor with all the other ingredients and process in short bursts until well combined. Do not purée the mixture. Alternatively, the salmon cubes may be minced with a knife to a uniform coarse texture.

Serve with toast points or crackers. Add a well-chilled champagne to complement this elegant appetizer.

Approximate preparation time: 20 minutes

Lapin Sauté aux Champignons

Serves 6

2 pounds fresh, boned, rabbit loin
Seasoned Flour:
    1 cup flour
    1 teaspoon white pepper
    ¼ teaspoon garlic powder
    1 teaspoon salt
2 eggs, lightly beaten
¼ cup butter
4 cloves garlic, minced
1 cup sliced mushrooms
¼ cup Oregon Chardonnay (or other dry white wine)
1 cup Brown Sauce (see Master Recipe)
¼ cup heavy cream
¼ cup chopped onion

    Clean and trim any fat or silver membrane from the boned rabbit loins. Place between two sheets of waxed paper and flatten with a mallet to approximately ¼ inch thick. Dredge (or thoroughly dust) the pieces in the seasoned flour and dip in the beaten egg.
    Heat the butter in a sauté pan until the foam subsides. Sauté the prepared rabbit pieces in the butter until golden brown on both sides. Add the garlic to the pan. Add the mushrooms to the pan and sauté for 3 minutes.
    Add the wine to deglaze, scraping the bottom and sides of the pan. Add the Brown Sauce and the cream. Stir constantly over high heat for approximately 1 minute until the sauce thickens slightly. Add the green onions and serve.

Approximate preparation time: 20 minutes

In early spring tiny wildflowers surround a Timberline trail marker. Rabbit, common in Europe, is gaining popularity in the United States. Once guests discover the delicious flavor of rabbit, a cross between veal and chicken, they ask for it again. Commercially grown rabbit, whole or in portions, can be found in local specialty grocery stores and markets.

Seafood Salad Coos Bay

Serves 6

    10 cups (about 3 bunches) fresh spinach, clean and dry
     3 hard-boiled eggs, chopped
     6 slices bacon, fried crisp and diced
5–6 ounces sea scallops, halved
5–6 ounces Pacific pink shrimp, cooked whole and peeled
     1 tablespoon butter
Dressing:
     grated zest and juice of 1 lemon
     ¼ cup Chardonnay or Riesling (or other dry white wine)
     ¼ cup white wine vinegar
    1½ cups olive oil
     1 tablespoon minced garlic
     1 tablespoon minced shallots
     1 tablespoon chopped fresh basil

Pacific pink shrimp, the tiny, flavorful shrimp used in this salad, are harvested by commercial fleets primarily based in the Oregon coastal towns of Coos Bay, Newport, and Astoria. These large, 90-foot trawlers spread their nets along the ocean floor, catching the crustaceans as they swim toward the surface. There are more than 300 varieties of shrimp in the world, but the Pacific pink shrimp is one of the smallest and most tender.

Wash, dry, and tear up the spinach, removing the stems.

Heat the dressing ingredients together. Before the dressing cools, toss the spinach, eggs, and bacon in enough dressing to lightly coat them. Arrange on plates and set aside.

Sauté the scallops and shrimp in butter. Arrange on top of the spinach and serve immediately.

Approximate preparation time: 20 minutes

Summer

Alpen Birchermuesli
Umpqua Summer Salad
Walla Walla Sweet Onion & Ham Tart
Trio of Summer Soups
Pacific Coast Halibut Sambal
Swedish Cream with Raspberry Sauce
Caramel Walnut Cookies
Tillamook Fruit Salad
Sauvie Island Creamy Gazpacho
Portland Pasta Salad
Sweet Cherry Tart
Mt. Hood Wildflower Salad
Sesame Ginger String Beans
Grilled King Salmon with Lime & Dill Butter

Alpen Birchermuesli

Serves 6

  6 crisp apples
  3 cups rolled oats, uncooked
1½ cups slivered almonds, toasted
  ¼ cup honey (or to taste)
1½ teaspoons vanilla extract
  1 cup heavy cream
  2 tablespoons wheat germ
  ¼ cup raisins

    garnish with any other fruits or nuts (optional)

    Mix the liquid ingredients together. Core and dice the apples. Mix with the oats, almonds, and liquid ingredients. Top with wheat germ and raisins. Garnish with some favorite fruits or nuts.

Approximate preparation time: 15 minutes

A popular summer breakfast with the staff and guests at Timberline Lodge, this hearty, centuries-old Swiss recipe is served with fresh fruits of the season.

Umpqua Summer Salad

This tantalizing salad combines the flavors of tiny shrimp, new potatoes, and crisp celery with the tangy taste of fresh summer apples. We often think of apples as an autumn fruit, but there are many delicious summer varieties grown around Milton-Freewater, and in the Hood River and Willamette valleys of Oregon. The juicy, distinctly flavored, green or red Gravensteins, the crisp Tydemans Red, or the green, maroon-blushed Paulared are but a few of the many kinds available beginning in early August.

Serves 6

  1 pound bay shrimp, cooked and peeled
  7 stalks celery, diced
  4 apples, cored and diced
  1 bell pepper, seeded and diced
  3 cups cooked red potatoes, diced
  ½ cup raisins, soaked in very hot water for 20 minutes and drained
  2 cups mayonnaise
    juice of 1 lemon
    salt and pepper to taste
  1 tablespoon fresh dill (or 2 teaspoons dried)
10–12 large, clean lettuce leaves for a bed

    garnish with hard-boiled egg slices

Toss together the shrimp, celery, apples, bell pepper, potato, and raisins. Mix the mayonnaise with the lemon juice and dill. Combine the dressing with the shrimp mixture, mixing thoroughly. Salt and pepper to taste. Serve on a bed of lettuce garnished with hard-boiled egg slices.

Approximate preparation time: 30 minutes

Concentric circles of sliced Walla Walla onions flavor this distinctive summer tart. Mild in flavor, these highly-prized yellow onions are grown in Washington's Walla Walla River Valley. Unlike the smaller commercial yellow onions, they do not store well and should be enjoyed whenever available throughout the summer months.

Walla Walla Sweet Onion & Ham Tart

Serves 8

3 medium Walla Walla sweet onions, thinly sliced
2 tablespoons butter
1 tablespoon caraway seed
8 ounces ham, diced
¼ cup flour
2 cups sliced mushrooms
½ cup cream
4 eggs
¼ cup apricot preserves
1 10-inch Tart Pastry (see Master Recipe)

In a large sauté pan, cook the onions in the butter for 20 minutes, or until golden brown. Add the caraway seeds, ham, and mushrooms. Sauté for 10 minutes, add the flour, and mix well. Remove from the heat.

Preheat the oven to 350°.

Beat the eggs and mix in the cream. Add to the onion mixture. Pour into an unbaked 10-inch tart shell. Bake at 350° for 30 to 45 minutes. Glaze by brushing heated apricot preserves over the top. Bake another 10 to 15 minutes. Cool. Serve in wedges.

Approximate preparation time: 30 minutes, 45 minutes to bake

Alpine wildflowers carpet the meadows of Cairn Basin, one of the most beautiful areas in the Mt. Hood wilderness. In early summer purple lupine adorn mountain roadsides, alpine trails, and the slopes surrounding Timberline Lodge.

Trio of Summer Soups

This trio of cool, summer soups offers guests at Timberline a variety of refreshing ways to begin any meal. For area-operator Richard Kohnstamm, these soups evoke memories of elegant and leisurely meals enjoyed as a young man on special occasions with his parents.

Alpenglow Berry Soup

Serves 8

2 cups buttermilk
1 cup plain yogurt
1 cup orange juice concentrate
2 cups sour cream
2 tablespoons honey

2 tablespoons fresh lemon or lime juice
dash of cinnamon
3 cups fresh sweet berries (e.g., blueberries, strawberries)

Mix together all the ingredients except the berries. Chill thoroughly. Wash and drain the berries. Be sure all hulls and stems are removed. Add the berries to each serving.

Approximate preparation time: 10 minutes

Champagne Strawberry Bisque

Serves 6–8

3 cups fresh strawberries
1½ cups sour cream
½ cup milk
1 cup champagne

¾ cup sugar
1 tablespoon vanilla extract
1 tablespoon lemon juice
1 teaspoon kirschwasser

garnish with fresh mint

Clean and hull the strawberries, reserving a few for the garnish. Combine the strawberries, sour cream, milk, champagne, sugar, vanilla, lemon juice, and kirschwasser. Purée in a food processor or blender. Chill. Garnish each serving with sliced strawberries and a mint leaf.

Approximate preparation time: 10 minutes

Chilled Danish Buttermilk Soup

Serves 8

1 quart buttermilk
½ cup sugar

1 lemon, juice and zest
¼ teaspoon cinnamon

In a mixing bowl, combine the buttermilk, sugar, lemon juice and zest, and cinnamon. Stir until sugar is dissolved. Chill thoroughly. Serve garnished with a thin slice of lemon floating on each serving.

Approximate preparation time: 10 minutes

Pacific Coast Halibut Sambal

Here is a simple and savory recipe for Pacific halibut. Its firm, mild-flavored white meat is ideal for baking, poaching, or grilling on a warm summer evening.

Serves 6

6 6-ounce portions of halibut fillet
Sambal Sauce:
    ¾ cup sour cream
    1½ tablespoons honey
    ½ teaspoon turmeric
    ½ teaspoon dry ground mustard
    ½ teaspoon cayenne pepper
    ½ teaspoon curry powder
        pinch of salt

garnish with sautéed tomatoes

Preheat the oven to 350°.
    To prepare the sauce, combine the sour cream and honey until smooth. Add the spices and salt, and mix until blended completely.
    Place the fillets on a lightly oiled cookie sheet. Brush with butter and sprinkle with salt and pepper. Bake at 350° for 10 to 15 minutes until done. Serve with Sambal Sauce and sautéed tomatoes for garnish.

Approximate preparation time: 30 minutes

Primarily an offshore fish, Pacific halibut is caught from boats drifting along the coast of Northern California to Alaska. In Oregon, Pacific City is a favorite spot to catch this 40 to 100 pound fish.

Swedish Cream with Raspberry Sauce

Serves 8

2 cups heavy cream
¾ cup sugar
1 tablespoon vanilla extract
1 tablespoon (1½ envelopes) unflavored gelatin
3 cups sour cream
Raspberry Sauce (see Master Recipe)

Combine the cream, sugar, vanilla, and unflavored gelatin in a sauce-pan. Heat until hot but not boiling. Remove from heat and stir in sour cream. Pour into serving dishes and chill until set, about 3 hours. Prepare the Raspberry Sauce and serve on top of the Swedish Cream. Alternatively, the Raspberry Sauce may be mixed into the Swedish Cream and the dessert served decorated with whipped cream.

Approximate preparation time: 15 minutes preparation, 3 hours until chilled

Note: Boysenberries, marion berries, or blackberries may be substituted for the raspberries.

When selecting fresh raspberries, remember they are delicate and highly perishable. Freshly picked raspberries have a lightly frosted appearance and should be rinsed quickly and carefully, if at all.

A simple and elegant dessert, this versatile cream goes well with any fruit sauce or purée. For variety try lightly blending two sauces with a spatula or knife into colorful swirls. Blackberries, marion berries, poached pears, peaches, or kiwi make delicious sauces, served individually or in combination with Swedish Cream.

Caramel Walnut Cookies

A perfect accompaniment to an elegant dessert or tucked into a child's lunch box, these delicious cookies have a chewy walnut filling. They keep well in a cookie jar, and can be frozen for special occasions.

Yield: 18 cookies

Dough:
   1 cup butter
   ½ cup sugar
   ½ cup dark corn syrup
   2 egg yolks
   2½ cups flour
      egg white for glaze
Filling:
   ½ cup confectioners sugar
   ¼ cup butter
   3 tablespoons dark corn syrup
   ½ cup chopped walnuts

To make the dough, cream the butter and sugar until light. Add the dark corn syrup and egg yolks. Blend well. Mix in the flour. Wrap and chill for about one hour.

To prepare the filling, combine the confectioners sugar, butter, and dark corn syrup in a small saucepan over medium heat. Bring to a boil. Remove from heat and stir in the chopped walnuts. Chill.

To bake, preheat the oven to 375°.

Form the dough into 18 balls by rolling each to the size of a walnut. Place the balls of dough on a greased cookie sheet. Bake 5 minutes. Remove the cookies from the oven. Divide the filling into 18 portions and press one portion into the center of each cookie.

Return the dough to the oven and continue baking another 10 minutes.

Approximate preparation time: 45 minutes

Tillamook Fruit Salad

Serves 6

Dressing:
- 1 cup sour cream
- 2 tablespoons honey
- 1½ teaspoons apple cider vinegar
- ¼ teaspoon vanilla extract
- 1 tablespoon poppy seeds

5–6 cups various prepared fresh fruits, see below
  large clean lettuce leaves to line the serving plates

  garnish with fresh mint leaves

To prepare a larger quantity of dressing, follow the preparation instructions below using the following quantities.

Yield: 5½ cups

- 1 quart sour cream
- 1 cup honey
- 2 tablespoons apple cider vinegar
- 1 teaspoon vanilla extract
- ¼ cup poppy seeds

To prepare the dressing, combine the first four ingredients in a food processor or blender and blend. Pour into a small container and mix in the poppy seeds. Set aside in the refrigerator.

The salad may be prepared with a variety of fruits depending on availability and individual taste. Melons such as honeydew, cantaloupe, and watermelon are suitable and attractive. They may be either cut into chunks or carved into balls with a melon baller. Berries of all kinds may be used in this salad, although if very soft berries such as raspberries are used, care should be taken not to crush them when the salad is mixed.

Toss the fruit in the dressing to coat all of the pieces. Arrange the lettuce leaves on individual serving plates. Arrange the fruit on the lettuce leaves. Garnish with fresh mint leaves and serve with sliced Tillamook cheddar cheese.

Approximate preparation time: 20 minutes

Summer at Timberline Lodge offers guests the thrill of glacier skiing on the Palmer snowfield, relaxing by the year-round swimming pool, or hiking along one of the more than 150 miles of trails surrounding Mt. Hood. Here, by the Lodge's pool, an assortment of fruits combines the color, textures, and tastes of summer. Poppy seeds give this salad dressing a fragrant, nutty flavor. The dressing goes well with all summer fruits as a dressing or dip.

Sauvie Island Creamy Gazpacho

Serves 8

1 cucumber, peeled and diced
1 green onion, minced
1 clove garlic, minced
1 bell pepper, diced
1 bunch parsley or cilantro, chopped
1 tablespoon honey
1 tablespoon chopped fresh dill (or 2 teaspoons dried)
4 cups tomato juice
1 cup sour cream and/or plain yogurt
   salt and pepper to taste
   juice of 2 lemons
½ cup olive oil

   garnish with 8 to 10 sliced mushrooms, fresh chives, watercress, or cilantro

   Combine all of the ingredients except the mushrooms in a food processor or blender and blend until smooth. Garnish with the sliced mushrooms and a few sprigs of dill, watercress, or cilantro.

Approximate preparation time: 15 minutes

A communal herb that grows in clumps, chives have an oniony taste and bright green color, making it an ideal garnish for this creamy variation of a classic Spanish soup. You can buy chives in most grocery stores and plant them in your garden where they will grow year after year.

In the rich, irrigated land of Treasure Valley in Eastern Oregon, a field of chives is in full bloom.

Portland Pasta Salad

Serves 6

Pesto:
> 1 bunch chopped fresh basil
> 1 clove garlic, peeled
> 1 tablespoon pine nuts
> ¼ cup chopped parsley
> ¼ cup grated Parmesan cheese
> 2 teaspoons olive oil

Vinaigrette:
> ¼ cup red wine vinegar
> 1 egg white
> ⅛ cup crumbled Feta cheese
> 1 cup olive oil
> salt and pepper to taste

Salad:
> 1 red bell pepper, cut into strips
> 1 tomato, cut into wedges
> 1 green onion, chopped
> ⅛ cup Greek olives (pitted and chopped or left whole)
> ¼ cup summer sausage (or salami) cut into julienne
> 1 quart cooked tricolor seashell pasta (2½ cups dry)

large, clean lettuce leaves as a plate liner
salt and pepper to taste

garnish with strips of sun-dried tomato and crumbled Feta

In a food processor or blender, blend all the pesto ingredients until smooth and creamy. To make the pesto vinaigrette, add the red wine vinegar, egg white, and Feta to the pesto, blending well. Add the oil and blend to combine. Season with salt and pepper to taste.

Combine all the salad ingredients and mix with the vinaigrette. Chill. Arrange on a bed of lettuce and garnish with sun-dried tomatoes and crumbled Feta cheese.

Approximate preparation time: 45 minutes

Basil, the main ingredient of pesto, is a member of the mint family. When fresh, its highly scented leaves have a fragrance similar to cloves and licorice. Dried, they have a subtle, curry flavor. Fresh basil, available during the summer months, should be chopped just before using to keep its crisp, pungent flavor.

The first summer fruit to show at the market is often the sweet cherry. Grown throughout the Northwest, the dark red Bing variety is the most popular. But be sure to try the other varieties: Lambert, with its rich flavor and bright red heart-shaped fruit or Rainier, the delicately flavored golden round cherry.

Sweet Cherry Tart

Serves 12

Tart Dough:
    2¾ cups flour
    1 teaspoon baking powder
    ⅔ cup sugar
    ½ cup chilled butter
    2 eggs
    ½ teaspoon vanilla extract
    8 ounces sliced almonds, toasted
Amaretto Cream:
    1 tablespoon water
    1 teaspoon almond extract
    1½ tablespoons (2¼ envelopes) unflavored gelatin
    4 ounces cream cheese
    ½ cup sour cream
    2 tablespoons half-and-half
    ¼ cup sugar
Cherry Topping:
    2 cups Pinot Noir (or other dry red wine)
    1 cup water
    ¼ cup sugar
    4 tablespoons cornstarch
    4 cups fresh, pitted Bing cherries

Preheat the oven to 350°.

To prepare the tart dough, combine the flour, baking powder, sugar, and butter in the bowl of a food processor. Process in short bursts until the mixture has a crumbly texture. (Or cut the butter into the dry ingredients, using a pastry cutter or two knives.) Add the eggs, vanilla, and almonds, and combine until just mixed (if using a food processor, process in bursts until a ball is formed).

Press the dough into a 9-inch tart pan with a removable bottom. Prick the surface of the dough using a fork. Line the pastry with aluminum foil filled with raw rice. Bake for 10 to 15 minutes. Remove the foil and continue baking until light-golden brown. Remove from the oven and pour in the Amaretto cream. Chill.

To make the Amaretto cream, combine the water, almond extract, and gelatin. Set aside. Cream the cream cheese, then add the sour cream, half-and-half, and sugar. Melt the gelatin by placing the bowl in very hot water. Stir until dissolved. Add the melted gelatin to the creamy mixture.

To prepare the cherry topping, combine the water, sugar, and cornstarch. Bring the wine to a boil in a saucepan, and stir in the cornstarch mixture. Cook until thickened. Add the cherries and heat briefly. Pour into the chilled tart and refrigerate until served.

Approximate preparation time: 5 hours, including chilling time

Mt. Hood Wildflower Salad with Hazelnut Vinaigrette

Both delicious and beautiful, this refreshing summer salad uses a variety of decorative and edible flowers. When making this salad, make sure any blossoms you pick are free of pesticides and roadside exhaust.

Serves 6

Salad:
   12 nasturtium blossoms
   24 borage blossoms
    6 garlic chive blossoms
    1 head butter lettuce
Vinaigrette:
   ½ cup hazelnut oil
   ¾ cup salad oil
   ½ cup toasted and skinned hazelnuts
   ¼ cup white wine vinegar
    1 teaspoon soy sauce
    1 teaspoon thyme leaves
       salt and pepper to taste
    1 egg white

To prepare the dressing, combine the two oils and set aside. Combine all the other vinaigrette ingredients in a food processor or blender. When thoroughly puréed, slowly blend in the oils. Makes about 2 cups.

To arrange the salad, rinse the flowers gently under cold running water. Divide the butter lettuce into individual leaves. Clean and dry the lettuce leaves. Arrange the small inner leaves in the centers of 6 salad plates. Place the larger leaves over the centers so that they form dome shapes.

Arrange the nasturtiums and garlic chive blossoms around the domes. Ladle a little vinaigrette on each salad and top with the borage blossoms.

Approximate preparation time: 30 minutes

Here are some edible varieties you might want to try:
   borage
   chive blossoms
   cornflowers
   daylilies
   lavender
   nasturtium blossoms & leaves
   pansies
   rose geraniums
   rose petals
   tulip petals
   violets
   zucchini blossoms

Sesame Ginger String Beans

Serves 6

1½ pounds fresh, trimmed string beans
    vegetable oil for deep frying
  4 tablespoons light sesame oil
1½ teaspoons minced fresh ginger
1½ teaspoons minced green onion
  2 medium cloves garlic, minced
  2 tablespoons minced ham
  2 tablespoons minced, prepared pickled radish (optional)
  2 teaspoons sugar
  2 teaspoons red wine vinegar
  2 tablespoons plus 1 teaspoon soy sauce
 ¼ cup Chicken Stock (see Master Recipe)
  2 teaspoons cornstarch

    garnish with toasted sesame seeds

To toast sesame seeds: Preheat the oven to 350°. Spread the seeds on a rimmed baking sheet and bake in the center of the oven for 12 minutes, or until golden brown. Watch carefully, and shake the pan several times while baking. The seeds may also be toasted in an ungreased skillet on the stove top. Since sesame seeds will turn rancid at room temperature, they should be refrigerated.

   Heat the oil until it is very hot. Blanch the beans in the hot oil for 30 seconds. Drain on paper towels. In a separate pan, sauté the ginger, green onion, garlic, ham, and radish for 4 minutes.

   Combine the sugar, vinegar, and soy sauce. Mix the Chicken Stock with the cornstarch. Add both liquid mixtures to the pan in which the ham mixture was sautéed and bring to a boil, stirring constantly. Add the string beans to the pan, heat, and coat with the sauce. Serve garnished with toasted sesame seeds.

Approximate preparation time: 15 minutes.

Note: Pickled radish is available in oriental grocery stores.

Fresh string beans should have firm, smooth pods that do not bend, but "snap". Experiment with varieties such as the stringless Oregon Blue Lake or the flavorful haricot vert, *a stringed French bean.*

Grilled King Salmon with Lime & Dill Butter

*Seasoned or **compound butters** are quick, tasty, and simple sauces. Be sure to use a good quality, fresh butter, preferably unsalted. Compound butters can be made ahead of time, spread on wax paper, tightly rolled, and stored in the freezer. "Rounds" can then be sliced off whenever needed.*

Serves 6

Lime and Dill Butter:
   1 cup butter
   2 teaspoons lime zest
   2 tablespoons fresh lime juice
   ¼ cup chopped fresh dill (or 3 tablespoons dried)
      salt and white pepper to taste
6 6-ounce portions salmon fillet
   salt and pepper

Place the Dill and Lime Butter ingredients in a mixer and whip until well mixed. Place in a pastry bag. Pipe rosettes onto waxed or parchment paper and chill.

Grill the salmon fillets for approximately 10 minutes on a side. Serve with a Lime and Dill Butter rosette on each serving.

Approximate preparation time: 30 minutes

Rich in flavor, the firm, orange-pink meat of the King, or Chinook, salmon is suitable for nearly any cooking method. Here it is simply grilled and served with a compound butter.

Autumn

Pinot Noir Poached Pears
Autumn Appetizers
Dill Egg Braid
Peanut Butter Pie Brandon
Breast of Chicken with Chanterelles
Wild Rose Hip Soup
Alpine Chocolate Pavé
Roast Saddle of Venison with Morels
Hood River Pear & Hazelnut Tart
Classic French Onion Soup
Seafood Warrenton

Pinot Noir Poached Pears with Crème Anglaise

This dramatic pear dessert rests on an original calendar celebrating the opening of Timberline Lodge in 1937.

Serves 6

6 fresh ripe pears, peeled and cored
2 cups Pinot Noir (or other dry red wine)
1 cup water
1 cup brown sugar
¼ teaspoon ground cardamom
2 whole cloves
1 cinnamon stick
Crème Anglaise (see Master Recipe)

garnish with fresh mint

In this recipe underripe fruit may be used. The long-stemmed Anjou pear, grown in the Hood River Valley, makes a delicious choice. Other varieties to try include the sweet Comice or the well-known Bartlett. Most people are familiar with the yellow Bartlett, but the burgundy-skinned Red Bartlett, pictured here, is another popular type that holds its shape when being cooked.

Peel and core the pears. The pears may be either left whole or cut in half lengthwise.

Place the pears in a saucepan just big enough to hold them. Add the water, wine, sugar, and spices. Cover and heat until the liquid is just at the boiling point. Poach the pears by maintaining this temperature for approximately 30 minutes, depending on the ripeness of the pears. They should be tender but not overcooked or mushy. Remove from the heat and let cool in the liquid overnight.

Serve with Crème Anglaise and garnish with a sprig of fresh mint.

Approximate preparation time: 45 minutes to prepare, marinate overnight

*Salmon, smoked with alderwood chips,
has a rich flavor and a dark flesh,
which combines well with the dill-
scented bread rounds.*

Autumn Appetizers

Alderwood Smoked Salmon Mousse

Serves 6

6 ounces smoked salmon
1 pound cream cheese
½ cup butter, melted
 juice of ½ lemon
¼ cup minced green onion

¼ cup heavy cream
4 tablespoons capers
2 teaspoons prepared horseradish
 pinch of white pepper

Whip the cream cheese in a mixer until soft. Slowly add the remaining ingredients. Whip until smooth. Chill until firm, approximately 1 hour. Serve with crackers, bread, or raw vegetables.

Approximate preparation time: 15 minutes to assemble, 1 hour to chill

Stuffed Mushrooms Aurora Colony

Serves 8

2 pounds mushrooms, medium-size
1 tablespoon butter
2 cloves garlic, minced
 salt and pepper to taste
¼ cup Oregon Chardonnay
 (or other dry white wine)
1 pound cream cheese

 garnish with chopped parsley

½ cup chopped parsley
1 teaspoon chopped fresh dill
 (or ½ teaspoon dried)
3–5 cloves garlic, minced
½ cup grated Parmesan cheese
½ cup fresh bread crumbs

Prized throughout Europe and North America for its delicious flavor, a boletus mushroom grows in the forest surrounding Timberline Lodge.

Preheat the oven to 400°.
Wipe the mushrooms clean with a dry paper towel. Remove the stems and set aside. Sauté the caps until soft. Set the caps aside to cool.
Mince the stems. Heat the butter to foaming in a sauté pan and add the 2 cloves of garlic. Add the minced mushroom stems, cook lightly, and season to taste with salt and pepper. Add the wine and cook lightly. Set aside to cool.
Combine the cream cheese, remaining minced garlic, parsley, and dill, mixing thoroughly. Add the sautéed stems, mixing well. Stuff the mushroom caps by spooning this mixture into the inverted caps.
Combine the Parmesan cheese and the bread crumbs. Sprinkle this mixture on top of the stuffed mushroom caps. Bake at 400° until hot and lightly browned. Garnish with chopped parsley.

Approximate preparation time: 30 minutes

Dill Egg Braid

Yield: two braided loaves

1 ounce active dry yeast
1 cup warm water (90°)
4 eggs, beaten
½ cup sugar
¼ cup butter, softened
1 cup finely minced fresh dill (or ¾ cup dried)
½ cup dry milk powder
1½ teaspoons salt
5–6 cups bread flour
    egg wash:
        1 egg yolk
        1 tablespoon water or milk

Combine the yeast and water, and allow to soften and bloom until it has a foamy appearance. In a large bowl, combine the yeast with the eggs, sugar, butter, dill, milk powder, and salt. When well mixed, begin adding the flour. Add the flour one cup at a time, mixing well after each addition. Turn onto a floured board and knead until smooth and elastic. Oil a large clean bowl and turn the dough in the bowl so that it is lightly coated with oil. Cover with a damp towel and let rise until double in bulk.

Preheat the oven to 350°.

Punch the dough down. Turn onto a lightly floured board. Divide the dough into 6 pieces and lightly knead each piece to remove any large air pockets.

Roll into long round pieces, approximately 1 inch in diameter. Braid into two braids of three strands each. Pinch the ends of the braided loaves and tuck under. Beat the egg yolk and water or milk together. Lightly brush the braids with the egg wash. Let rise until doubled. Bake at 350° until golden brown, about 45 minutes.

Approximate preparation time: 3 hours

Note: This bread can be frozen after being brushed with egg wash. Thaw, let rise, and bake at a later date.

Peanut Butter Pie Brandon

Serves 8

Crust:
- ¾ cup unsalted peanuts, skinned and finely chopped
- 1 cup graham cracker crumbs
- ¼ cup brown sugar
- ¼-⅓ cup melted butter

Chocolate filling layer:
- ½ cup butter, softened
- ¾ cup confectioners' sugar
- 1 egg at room temperature
- 3½ ounces chocolate, melted (semi-sweet or milk chocolate)
- 1 teaspoon vanilla extract

Peanut butter filling:
- 8 ounces cream cheese
- ½ cup creamy peanut butter
- 2 tablespoons granulated sugar
- ¼ cup butter, softened
- ½ cup heavy cream
- 1 tablespoon vanilla extract
- 1 cup Ganache (see Master Recipe)

garnish with chopped peanuts

To finely chop nuts: *Use either the quick, on-off action of your food processor, or place the nuts on a cutting board and use a long, heavy French chef's knife to rapidly chop in an up-and-down motion, pushing the chopped nut pieces into a pile until the desired uniform size is reached.*

To prepare the crust, combine the ingredients, adding enough melted butter to bind the ingredients together. Press into a greased 9-inch tart pan with a removable bottom. Chill.

Prepare the chocolate layer by creaming the butter and sugar until fluffy. Mix in the egg. Add the melted chocolate, scraping the bowl well. Add the vanilla. Continue mixing until fluffy. Spread into a smooth layer in the bottom of the chilled crust. Chill.

For the peanut butter layer, cream all the ingredients except the cream and vanilla. Scraping the bowl often, cream until light. Whip the cream and vanilla until stiff. Fold into the peanut butter mixture. Spread this mixture in a mound on top of the chocolate layer. Chill.

Pour warm Ganache over the chilled pie. Sprinkle with a few chopped peanuts. Remove the ring from the tart pan. Chill for approximately 2 hours.

Approximate preparation time: 45 minutes, 2 hours chilling time

Named after a pastry chef at Timberline who developed it, this scrumptious pie offers a delicious twist on two old favorites: peanut butter and chocolate! A favorite of children and adults, this dessert is good any time of year.

Breast of Chicken with Chanterelles

The original drawing of an Indian chief in headdress that is carved on the entrance door to the ski lodge serves as a backdrop for this autumn dish. The beads below the face are actually initials of some of those instrumental in the design of the Lodge.

Serves 6

6 skinless, boneless chicken breasts (about 5 ounces each)
   vegetable oil spray
Sauce:
   1 tablespoon chopped onion
   1 clove garlic, minced
   2 tablespoons butter
   ¾ pound fresh chanterelles (or substitute white mushrooms)
   1 teaspoon marjoram
   ½ cup sherry (use good quality dry sherry)
     salt and pepper to taste
   1 cup butter, softened

Season both sides of the chicken breasts with the salt and pepper. Place the chicken breasts on a hot grill sprayed with vegetable oil (or sauté in a pan with butter). Turn the breasts every 3 or 4 minutes. Cook until firm but not dried out.

In a separate pan, sauté the onion and garlic until the onion is translucent. Do not let the garlic brown. Add the chanterelles and marjoram, and lightly sauté. Season with salt and pepper.

Deglaze the pan with sherry and simmer until the liquid has reduced by half. Whisk in the soft butter a little at a time until well combined. Check the seasoning and keep the sauce warm until needed.

To serve, slice the chicken breasts and fan out the slices. Top with the chanterelle and sherried butter sauce.

Approximate preparation time: 30 minutes

Chanterelles are one of the most delicious of the wild Northwest mushrooms. Available in the autumn, these trumpet shaped fungi can be found by mushroom seekers alongside a forest trail, or in most Northwest markets. Any dirt or debris on mushrooms can be carefully brushed off or wiped with a towel; it is not necessary to rinse them.

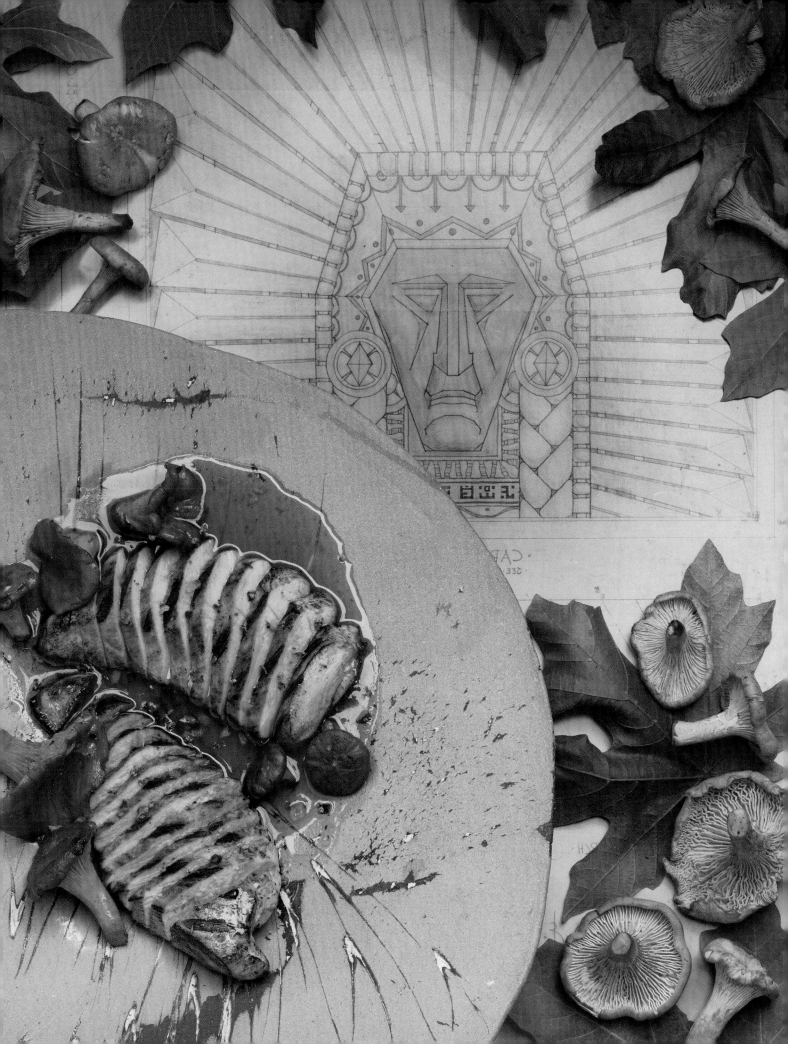

Wild Rose Hip Soup

Serves 8

4 ounces rose hip powder (finely milled)
8 cups water
1 cup sugar
   juice of 1 lemon
¼ cup Raspberry Sauce (see Master Recipe)
¼ cup cornstarch
¼ cup cold water

   garnish with sweetened whipped cream flavored with vanilla, and toasted slivered almonds

After the first frost had turned the green fruit of the wild rose to a brilliant red, Northwest Indians would gather rose hips to use in a number of ways: a cure for colic, a remedy for colds, and an elixir for pain. Today, guests at Timberline Lodge take pleasure in this tasty soup made from finely milled rose hip powder.

In a saucepan, bring the rose hip powder, water, and sugar to a boil. Reduce heat to a simmer and cook for 30 minutes.

Remove from the heat and let the rose hip sediment settle. Decant the liquid off the top or strain through a coffee filter into another saucepan. Return the liquid to the heat. Bring to a boil and thicken with the cornstarch mixed in water. Let it cool, then add the lemon juice and Raspberry Sauce. Garnish with a dollop of sweetened and flavored whipped cream. Sprinkle a few toasted almonds on top of the cream and serve.

Approximate preparation time: 1 hour

Note: Rose hip powder is available in natural foods stores.

This classic French recipe is as delicious
as it is simple to make. Translated in
French, pavé means "paving brick" and
refers to the shape of the dessert.

Alpine Chocolate Pavé

Yield: 24 pieces

 2 cups raisins
 2 cups toasted, skinned, and chopped hazelnuts
 ½ cup rum or brandy
2½ cups flour
1½ teaspoons salt
1½ teaspoons baking soda
1½ cups brown sugar
 1 cup water
 2 cups butter
12 ounces good quality semi-sweet chocolate
  (or 2 cups semi-sweet chocolate chips)
 4 eggs
 2 cups milk
 1 recipe Ganache (see Master Recipe)
 1 12-inch pan

To prepare this recipe for a party of 50, use the following quantities:

 4 cups raisins
 4 cups hazelnuts
 1 cup rum or brandy
 5 cups flour
 1 tablespoon salt
 3 teaspoons baking soda
 3 cups brown sugar
 2 cups water
 4 cups butter
24 ounces good quality semi-sweet chocolate
  (or 4 cups semi-sweet chocolate chips)
 8 eggs
 4 cups milk
 1 double recipe Ganache (see Master Recipe)
 1 17¾-inch by 25¾-inch by 2-inch pan

The weather worn trail sign in the photograph was the original marker used on the Blossom Trail that led hikers up the mountain in the 1930s.

Preheat the oven to 350°.

Place the raisins and hazelnuts in the brandy to soak.

Sift together the flour, salt, and baking soda. Combine the brown sugar, water, and butter in a saucepan and bring to a boil. Remove from the heat. Add the chocolate to the sugar mixture and stir until melted. Mix in the eggs one at a time. Alternately add the dry ingredients and the milk to the chocolate mixture.

Add the soaked raisins and nuts. Pour the batter into the baking pan and bake at 350° for 25 minutes. Let cool slightly before glazing. Glaze with Ganache. If the Ganache has been chilled, warm it slightly to loosen.

Approximate preparation time: 45 minutes

Roast Saddle of Venison with Morels

Venison is one game meat that is available to the nonhunter as well as the hunter. Most specialty meat stores carry commercially bred venison from New Zealand. At the Lodge it is served with a rich Madeira sauce and freshly picked wild morels.

Serves 6

2 pounds venison loin
  salt and pepper to taste
2 tablespoons oil
2 tablespoons butter
4 shallots, sliced
2 cups morel mushrooms, sliced
¼ cup Pinot Noir (or other dry red wine)
4 cups Madeira Sauce (see Master Recipe)

Preheat the oven to 450°.
Remove any of the silver skin from the venison loin. Rub with salt and pepper. Brown in the oil. Remove to a roasting pan. Roast at 450° for 20 to 30 minutes. Remove the loin from the pan and set aside in a warm place.
Add the butter and shallots to the roasting pan and roast for 15 minutes. Add the morels and roast for another 10 minutes. Deglaze the pan with wine. Add the Madeira Sauce and simmer for 15 minutes. Slice the loin into medallions. Serve with morel sauce.

Approximate preparation time: 1½ hours

Hood River Pear & Hazelnut Tart

Serves 8

  3 ounces almond paste
  2 eggs
  ½ cup butter, softened
  ⅓ cup sugar
  1 teaspoon vanilla extract
4½ ounces (about ¾ cup) ground, toasted hazelnuts
  1 9-inch tart pan lined with Tart Pastry (see Master Recipe)
    about ½ cup Ganache (see Master Recipe)
  3 Hood River Anjou pears (or 10 to 12 apricots), poached and sliced
    about ½ cup sugar
3–4 ounces apricot preserves

When selecting pears, remember that they are one of the few fruits that are picked before they ripen. It is best to let them mature at room temperature. A pear is ripe when its neck yields to gentle pressure.

Preheat the oven to 350°.

Cream the almond paste, gradually adding the eggs, butter, and sugar. Mix in the vanilla and then add the nuts.

Prepare the Tart Pastry and line a 9-inch tart pan. Spread Ganache over the bottom of the tart shell. Then smooth the almond paste mixture over the top of that. Arrange the poached, sliced pears or apricots over the top. Sprinkle with sugar.

Bake at 350° for 40 minutes. While the tart is still hot, glaze the top with apricot preserves. Let cool and serve.

Approximate preparation time: 1 hour

Note: This tart is equally successful using poached peaches, plums, or any seasonal fruit.

To poach fruit: In a deep saucepan, cook the fruit in simmering hot sugar syrup until tender. Remove the fruit and allow it to cool at room temperature. The sugar syrup is made by combining 1 cup of sugar and 2 cups of water (1:2 ratio) with the juice of a small lemon to discourage discoloration.

Classic French Onion Soup

Serves 8

8 cups thinly sliced onions
½ cup butter
2 tablespoons honey
½ cup Pinot Noir (or other dry red wine)
1 teaspoon thyme
½ teaspoon black pepper
½ teaspoon granulated garlic (or garlic powder)
8 cups Beef Stock (see Master Recipe)
1 teaspoon salt

garnish with a large crouton, Gruyère cheese, and grated Parmesan

Place the onions in a stockpot with the butter. Slowly cook the onions 30 to 45 minutes, or until they reach a deep golden brown. Add the honey, red wine, thyme, pepper, garlic, and stock.

Simmer the soup 30 to 40 minutes and salt to taste.

Serve au gratin style, with a large crouton placed on the soup, then covered with a slice of Gruyère cheese and grated Parmesan. Brown in a very hot oven until golden.

Approximate preparation time: 2 hours

To make the job of slicing onions less tearful, cooks have tried many methods, from paring the bulb under water to chilling it overnight. Whatever methods you use, a sharp, well-balanced knife does the job faster and easier.

One of the world's most renowned soups, and a favorite at the Lodge, this hearty onion soup makes an impressive first course or a substantial entrée.

Seafood Warrenton

The flavorful sauce used in this distinctive dish is made by deglazing the pan in which the shrimp and apples have been sautéed.

Serves 6

4–6 tablespoons butter
12 whole, peeled prawns, raw
¾ cup (about 4 ounces) bay shrimp
¾ cup (about 4 ounces) whole raw bay scallops
¾–1 pound white fish, such as cod, sole, or snapper, diced
2 apples, cored and sliced
1 teaspoon salt
1 teaspoon pepper
4–5 cloves garlic, minced
½ cup apple schnapps
½ cup hazelnut liqueur
2 cups apple juice
2½ tablespoons cornstarch
½ cup crushed hazelnuts

garnish with 3 sautéed apple slices per serving

Sauté the seafood and the apples in the butter. Season with salt, pepper, and garlic. Deglaze the pan with the apple and hazelnut liqueurs. Mix the apple juice and cornstarch, and add to the pan. Allow to boil for one minute. Spoon over rice and serve.

Approximate preparation time: 30 minutes

To deglaze: *After the food has been sautéed, remove it and any excess butter or fat from the pan. Add the required liquid to the pan, scraping and stirring the concentrated particles and juices from the sides and bottom of the pan into the liquid.*

Winter

Oregon Hazelnut Gâteau
Astoria Clam Chowder
Medallions of Beef Oregon Blue
Dungeness Crab with Sauce Verte
Glazed Vegetables
Timberline Ale & Cheese Soup
Onion Cheddar Rolls
Timberline Mountain-Style Chili
Cranberry & Sour Cream Muffins
Roast Oregon Duck with Huckleberries
Willamette Pilaf
Coastal Mist Cranberry Relish
Chocolate Decadence

Oregon Hazelnut Gâteau

Makes 1 Gâteau, serves 16-18

1 recipe Tart Pastry (see Master Recipe)
Filling:
    1½ cups sugar
    ⅓ cup hot water
    1 tablespoon lemon juice
    1 cup heavy cream (scalded)
    1 cup or 2 sticks butter (room temperature)
    ¼ cup honey (room temperature)
    3 cups or 12 ounces hazelnuts, toasted, skinned, chopped fine
Chocolate Mousse and Glaze:
    1 recipe Ganache (see Master Recipe)
    2½ cups heavy cream (chilled)
Decoration:
    2 ounces white chocolate (warmed)
      whipped cream and whole hazelnuts, toasted, skinned

Virtually all the hazelnuts grown in North America come from the fertile Willamette Valley of Oregon. Hazelnuts, also known as filberts, have a rich, nutty flavor that complements the dense chocolate gâteau pictured in the Lodge museum. The wrought iron beaver andirons, crafted by WPA workers in 1937, are used in the fireplaces of the guest bedrooms.

Day 1. Prepare one Tart Pastry recipe. To prepare filling, combine sugar, water, and lemon juice in a heavy saucepan. Bring to boil, stirring to dissolve sugar. Cook to caramel stage. (320°). Toward the end, turn heat to low to avoid burning the sugar. It should be a golden color. Remove from heat. Scald cream, carefully adding small amounts and whisking in each time. Whisk in butter. Simmer and stir until smooth. Stir in honey and nuts and cool.

    Preheat oven to 350°.

    To prepare the tart, separate one-third of pastry dough from the remainder. Roll into a circle just larger than a 10- to 12-inch tart pan (with removable bottom). Using the ring, cut dough for top. Set aside. Roll the remaining dough into a circle large enough to line pan with a 1-inch overlap. Do not stretch dough. Let overlap hang over gently. Place cooled filling in the bottom and put the top over the filling. Brush egg whites over the top, and seal the overlap to it. Egg wash top and dock with 10 ¼-inch cuts.

    Bake 35-40 minutes on a sheet pan on the bottom shelf with an empty sheet pan on the next shelf up. When tart is golden brown, remove from oven. Place a slightly weighted, flat pan on top of tart to flatten. When cool, place in the freezer overnight.

Day 2. To assemble Gâteau, prepare one recipe Ganache. Place frozen tart upside down on pan. Slightly cool 1½ cups Ganache. Whip heavy cream to firm, moist peaks. Reserve ¾ cup for garnish. Fold cooled, but still-liquid, Ganache into whipped cream. Place mousse on tart bottom. Chill until set. Slowly heat remaining 2 cups of Ganache to liquid. Pour over mousse and tart, covering the edges. Garnish by drizzling warmed white chocolate over top. Chill. Cut into 16-18 pieces, using a hot, dry knife. Garnish with whipped cream and hazelnuts.

Approximate preparation time: 4 hours over 2 days.

To toast hazelnuts, and to remove their outer skins: *Place the nuts on a baking sheet at 350° for about 15 minutes, or until they turn golden brown. Then, place the nuts in a terry cloth hand towel. Fold the towel and allow the nuts to "steam" for 5 minutes. Rub the towel firmly between your hands. This will cause most of the skins to flake off.*

Astoria Clam Chowder

Many Oregonians like to go clamming on their weekends at the coast where they dig for tender butter or steamer clams.

Serves 6-8

4 pounds fresh clams in the shell (or 3 cups of canned clams and juice)
1 cup chopped celery
1 medium onion, chopped
1 bell pepper, seeded and chopped
½ cup butter
2 strips bacon, diced
1 teaspoon thyme
½ cup flour
4 cups milk
2 cups red potatoes, diced
1 teaspoon salt
¼ teaspoon white pepper

For a recipe that yields approximately 10 gallons, you may wish to use the canned clams rather than the fresh, steamed clams. Follow the preparation instructions below and use the following quantities:

4 bunches celery, chopped
12 medium onions, chopped
12 bell peppers, seeded and chopped
2 pounds butter
1 pound bacon, diced
2 handfuls thyme
12 cups flour
4 gallons milk
4 46-ounce cans clam juice
4 46-ounce cans clams, chopped
7 pounds red potatoes, diced
　salt and white pepper to taste
　(approximately 4 handfuls salt and 2 handfuls pepper)

The waters of the Pacific Northwest are also inhabited by the world's largest clams, the geoducks, which can weigh from 3 to 7 pounds. Because of their size, geoducks (pronounced "gooey-ducks") are commercially harvested for canned clam chowder.

　Steam the fresh clams in 2 cups water. When they open, remove the meat from the shells and chop. Set aside. Strain the broth, being careful to discard any sand, and set aside.
　Sauté the celery, onions, and bell pepper in the butter until soft. Fry the bacon and add it, with the drippings, to the vegetables. Season with thyme. Sprinkle the flour over the sautéed vegetables and cook for 3 minutes, stirring constantly. Set aside.
　Bring the milk to a boil with the potatoes, clam broth, and clams. Add the liquid to the vegetable mixture, stirring constantly to prevent lumping. Season to taste. Return the soup to a boil and simmer for 30 minutes to cook the potatoes. Thin with milk if desired. Serve when ready.

Approximate preparation time: 1½ hours

*The earliest pioneers included cattlemen
who drove their herds across the sage-
strewn vastness of Oregon's inland empire.
Prized beef is still raised in the high
country desert east of the Cascades. In
this recipe tender medallions of beef
are served with a rich blue-cheese sauce.*

Medallions of Beef Oregon Blue

Serves 6

6 6-ounce beef tenderloin medallions
¼ cup butter
1 cup sliced onion
¾ cup heavy cream
2 tablespoons chopped parsley
1 tablespoon chopped chives
½ cup crumbled Oregon Blue cheese

   garnish with 1 teaspoon of the crumbled Blue cheese

In a large pan sauté the beef medallions in butter until browned on each side, approximately 6 minutes to a side. Remove from the pan. Add the sliced onions and sauté for 3 minutes. Add the cream. Cook over medium high heat until reduced by half. Add the parsley, chives, and crumbled Blue cheese. Stir until well combined. Pour over the medallions. Garnish with 1 teaspoon of crumbled Blue cheese for each serving.

Approximate preparation time: 30 minutes

Winters in Central Oregon are cold and dry while Timberline Lodge wears a blanket of snow. West of the Cascade Range moist marine air keeps temperatures mild, ensuring abundance in the coming seasons.

Dungeness Crab with Sauce Verte

Serves 6

3 whole, fresh, cooked, cleaned Dungeness crabs
Sauce Verte:
   1 bunch green onions, chopped
   ½ bunch parsley, chopped
     juice of 1½ lemons
   3 dashes of Worcestershire sauce
   3 dashes of Tabasco sauce (or other red pepper sauce)
   2 tablespoons water
   2 cups mayonnaise
     salt and pepper to taste

To make the sauce verte, combine all the ingredients in a food processor or blender and purée until smooth. Serve as a dipping sauce with the chilled, cracked crab.

Approximate preparation time: 10 minutes

Named after an area on the Olympic Peninsula in Washington, Dungeness crabs are caught from Northern California to Alaska. When buying a whole crab, be sure that the shell is hard. As a crab matures, it sheds, or molts, its old shell and grows a larger one. The new shell is soft, and the meat is sparse. For some, part of the fun is cracking the crab. Or, buy one pound of crab meat to feed four.

Glazed Vegetables

An appliqué banner provides the background for this elegant, oriental presentation of glazed winter vegetables. The banner's title, Hunger Moon, comes from the Indian name for February.

Serves 6

1½–2 pounds of firm root vegetables, such as carrots, turnips, or rutabaga
   3 tablespoons butter
   2 tablespoons sugar
    water
    salt

    garnish with chopped parsley (or any favorite herb for color)

Carve the vegetables into smooth oval shapes of approximately equal size. The finished pieces should be about the size and shape of a whole date. Bring a pot of lightly salted water to a boil. Cook the vegetables firm but tender, 10 to 15 minutes. Drain the vegetables, reserving the cooking liquid. Plunge the vegetables into very cold water to stop the cooking process and to retain the bright color.

Reduce about 2 cups of the cooking liquid by half over a high heat.

Melt the butter with sugar in a sauté pan. Add ¾ cup of the reduced vegetable stock and cook over a high heat until reduced and syrupy.

Add the vegetables, shaking the pan until they are hot, evenly coated, and a glossy light-golden color.

Sprinkle with fresh herbs as desired.

Approximate preparation time: 30 minutes

Friends of Timberline, an organization formed to preserve and restore the furnishings and artwork of the Lodge, commissioned a banner for each month to be displayed on the massive fireplace in the lower lobby entrance.

Timberline Ale & Cheese Soup

Serves 8

    2 cups Chicken Stock (see Master Recipe)
    2 cups half-and-half
    1 cup Timberline Classic Ale (or other fine ale)
    2 cups grated Tillamook cheddar cheese
    ¼ cup flour
    ¼ cup butter
    salt and pepper to taste

Oregon's famous Tillamook cheddar cheese combines flavorfully with Timberline Classic Ale from one of Oregon's many micro-breweries.

Melt the butter in a soup pot and add the flour. Cook 5 to 10 minutes, stirring frequently. Be careful not to let it burn.

Add the Chicken Stock and ale, and cook another 10 to 15 minutes. Reduce the heat to a simmer. Add the half-and-half and cheese. Stir at once so that the cheese does not settle on the bottom of the pot and burn. Season with salt and pepper, and serve.

Approximate preparation time: 1 hour

After the Lodge was first opened, amateur woodcarvers were permitted to leave their initials on the wooden tables in the Blue Ox Bar—a much better surface than the splendid wooden building! One of these tables is used as the backdrop for this hearty, winter soup.

Onion Cheddar Rolls

Yield: 30 rolls

    1 cup warm (90°) water
    1 ounce (1 package) active dry yeast
    2 tablespoons dry milk powder
  1¾ cups bread flour
    ¾ cup sugar
    ¼ cup potato granules (or ½ cup leftover mashed potatoes)
    ½ cup finely chopped onion
    1 teaspoon salt
  10 egg yolks
    6 tablespoons water
    ½ cup butter
    6 ounces cream cheese
    ¾ cup grated Cheddar cheese
5½–6 cups bread flour (or all-purpose flour)
     egg wash:
       1 egg
       1 tablespoon water

Spectacular mountain scenery greets downhill skiers at Timberline, with over two dozen alpine trails that traverse miles of open snowfields and wind through snow-frosted forests.

Combine the warm water and yeast in a large bowl. Allow to rest about 20 minutes until it begins to take on a foamy appearance. Add the milk powder and 1¾ cups bread flour, and mix. Cover the bowl with a damp towel and set aside at room temperature for 1 hour.

Combine the sugar, potato granules, onion, salt, egg yolks, water, butter, Cheddar, and cream cheese, and add to the flour mixture. Mix well, adding the flour to form a stiff dough, one that will not flatten or spread. Knead the dough until it has a springy quality, like chewing gum.

Clean the bowl. Return the dough to it. Cover and let rise until double in bulk.

Punch down the dough and divide it into 30 portions. Shape into desired roll shape. Beat together the egg and water, and lightly brush onto the rolls. Let rise. Preheat the oven and bake at 350° until golden brown, about 8-10 minutes.

Approximate preparation time: 3 hours

Note: These rolls can be frozen after being brushed with egg wash and, at a later date, thawed, allowed to rise, and baked.

Timberline Mountain-Style Chili

Serves 8

    4 cups dry red beans
1½ pounds ground beef, coarse grind
    ½ cup diced onion
    3 tablespoons oil
    2 tablespoons salt (or to taste)
    8 cloves garlic, minced
1½ teaspoons oregano
1½ teaspoons ground cumin
    5 tablespoons chili powder
    1 pound canned tomatillos, crushed
    1 pound canned red tomatoes, diced
    8 cups rich, strong Beef Stock (see Master Recipe)

garnish with grated Cheddar cheese, cooked bacon strips, and chopped raw onions

Soak the red beans overnight in plenty of water.

Sauté the ground beef and onions together in the oil. Add spices, tomatillos, tomatoes, and cook for 10 minutes. Add the stock and drained beans. Bring to a boil. Reduce heat and simmer 1 hour, or until beans are cooked.

Remove 3 cups of chili and purée in a food processor or blender. Return the purée to the pot to thicken the chili. Serve hot, topped with garnishes.

Approximate preparation time: 2 hours to cook, overnight to soak the beans

This traditional chili recipe is perfect for a small fireside gathering, or a large après-ski crowd.

Cranberry & Sour Cream Muffins

Yield: 20 muffins

1½ cups butter
3 cups sugar
6 eggs
1 tablespoon vanilla extract
5¼ cups flour
3 teaspoons baking soda
½ teaspoon salt
3 teaspoons baking powder
3 cups sour cream
2½ cups chopped fresh cranberries
½ cup sour cream
    sliced almonds for topping (optional)

Cream the butter and sugar until light and fluffy. Add the eggs one by one, beating after each addition. Add the vanilla. Set aside.

Sift together the flour, baking soda, salt, and baking powder.

Alternately add the dry ingredients and the sour cream to the butter mixture. Dust the cranberries with a little flour and fold them into the batter.

Line the muffin tins with paper liners and fill ¾ full with batter. Place 1 teaspoon of sour cream on top of each unbaked muffin. Top with sliced almonds if desired. Bake at 350° for approximately 20 minutes, or until done.

Approximate preparation time: 45 minutes

Note: Any seasonal fruit, such as huckleberries, cherries, blueberries, or sweetened, chopped apples may be substituted.

A basket of warm cranberry muffins with sour cream centers rests on one of the hooked rugs made for the Lodge during its construction in 1936. Hand-hooked by WPA workers from discarded wool blankets that were dyed various colors before being cut into strips, these rugs were used in the common areas and guest rooms. Reproductions of these rugs are used today.

Roast Oregon Duck with Huckleberries

Indians from the Warm Springs Reservation still harvest the wild huckleberries that are used at Timberline Lodge.

Serves 4–6

2 ducklings
    salt and pepper
Huckleberry Sauce: (about 2 cups)
    4 cups veal stock or Chicken Stock (see Master Recipe)
    2 cups huckleberries
    ½ cup port
    1 tablespoon red wine vinegar
    2 tablespoons cornstarch
    2 tablespoons cold water
    2 tablespoons honey
    salt and pepper to taste

A diminutive relative of the cultivated blueberry, the huckleberry is found growing underneath the Douglas firs of the Cascade forests. Many Oregonians return to their secret picking spots every August or September to harvest this tasty blue-black berry.

To roast the ducks, preheat the oven to 425°.

Season the ducks inside and out by sprinkling with salt and pepper. Place on a rack in a preheated roasting pan. Roast the ducks 45 minutes at 425°. As the ducks are roasting, turn them a ¼ turn every 15 minutes. Pricking the skin with a fork will allow some of the excess fat to run off in the roasting. From time to time, remove the excess fat from the roasting pan with a bulb baster.

After 45 minutes, reduce the heat to 350° and continue roasting, uncovered, an additional 45 minutes.

Check for doneness by making a small cut into the meat where the thigh joins the body. The juices that escape should run clear.

Remove the ducks from the oven and allow to rest until cool enough to touch. Split each duck in half lengthwise using a sharp knife or poultry shears. Remove the rib bones. They should be easy to pull out.

Reheat the ducks in the oven for 5 to 10 minutes at 425° to crisp the skin. Serve with the Huckleberry Sauce.

To prepare the huckleberry sauce while the duck is roasting, bring the port to a boil and reduce by half. Add the huckleberries, stock, and vinegar. Bring to a boil and simmer uncovered for 30 minutes. Purée the sauce, return it to the stove, and continue simmering. Mix the cornstarch and water. While stirring, add enough of the mixture to the sauce to thicken it slightly so that it reaches a syrupy consistency.

Simmer another 20 minutes, adjust the seasoning, and serve with the reheated duck.

Approximate preparation time: 2 hours

Willamette Pilaf

Serves 6

½ cup currants
½ onion, minced
 1 carrot, minced
 1 stalk celery, minced
 8 mushrooms, sliced
   salt and pepper to taste
¼ cup Oregon Chardonnay (or other dry white wine)
 4 tablespoons butter
¾ cup raw white rice cooked with:
   ¾ cup tomato juice
   ¾ cup lightly salted water
¾ cup wild rice cooked with:
   ¼ cup Oregon Chardonnay (or other dry white wine)
    1 teaspoon marjoram
   1¼ cup lightly salted water
½ cup coarsely chopped hazelnuts

Cover currants with boiling water and soak for 15 minutes.

Sauté the vegetables and mushrooms in butter until tender. Season with salt and pepper. Deglaze the pan with wine. Mix the rices with the hazelnuts and drained currants. Add to the vegetables and serve hot.

Approximate preparation time: 1 hour

Glowing trees and festive caroling fill the Timberline lobby at Christmastime, while children await a visit from Santa Claus and his team of matching reindeer. Christmas Eve dinner in the candlelit Cascade Dining Room is a tradition that many local families and visitors look forward to each year.

Coastal Mist Cranberry Relish

Serves 8

1 orange
3 cups whole fresh cranberries
1 cup sugar
 juice of ½ lemon
½ cup port or other sweet wine

Taking the whole orange, grate the skin onto a piece of waxed paper, being careful to remove only the orange outer layer, or zest. Squeeze the juice from the orange and set aside.

Coarsely grind the cranberries in a food processor or food grinder. Add the orange juice, zest, and the remaining ingredients. Cover the relish and let it stand in the refrigerator for two days before serving. If the relish is needed sooner, simmer it for 20 minutes and chill before serving.

Approximate preparation time: 15 minutes preparation, 2 days of marinating

This zesty relish makes an excellent accompaniment for poultry, game, baked ham, or smoked meats. Grown in wet, spongy bogs along the southern coasts of Oregon and Washington, the tart, red cranberry is available fresh from autumn to early winter.

Chocolate Decadence

Serves 8

Cake:
  1 pound semi-sweet chocolate
  ½ cup plus 2 tablespoons butter
  6 eggs
  1 tablespoon sugar
  1 tablespoon flour
Topping:
  2 cups heavy cream
  1 teaspoon vanilla extract
  ¼ cup confectioners sugar
1 square semi-sweet chocolate for chocolate curls
Raspberry Sauce (see Master Recipe)

Preheat the oven to 425°.
Prepare an 8-inch cake pan by lining the bottom with a circle of parchment paper.
In a double boiler, melt the chocolate and butter. In another mixing bowl, combine the eggs and sugar, and place in a hot water bath. Heat this mixture, stirring until warm (approximately 120°). Using a mixer, whip the egg mixture at high speed until double in volume, approximately 10 minutes.
Gently fold the flour into the egg mixture. Add the chocolate mixture, folding in gently. Pour into the prepared cake pan. Bake 10 minutes. Remove from the oven and cool. Freeze overnight.
To remove the frozen cake from the pan, heat the pan briefly and turn it upside down over a cake plate. Remove and discard parchment paper. Whip the cream with vanilla and sugar to taste. Fill a pastry bag, fitted with a decorative tip, with some of the whipped cream. Generously cover the cake with the rest of the whipped cream and smooth with a palette knife. Pipe rosettes on top of the cake. Make chocolate curls by shaving the slightly warmed chocolate square with a vegetable peeler. Decorate with the chocolate curls using one curl per slice. Pour Raspberry Sauce over each slice before serving.

Approximate preparation time: 45 minutes, overnight to freeze

A Timberline Classic. Photographed in the main lobby beside curled andirons, made from railroad rails, is the ultimate chocolate lover's dessert. Raspberry sauce, made from the summer bounty of frozen berries, is a refreshing reminder of warm days to come.

Soft winter snows blanket the southern flanks of Mt. Hood, a favorite area for cross-country skiers.

Tart Pastry

3½ cups flour (A.P. or pastry)
 ¼ cup sugar
 1 cup or 2 sticks butter (chilled)
 2 large eggs
   about ⅓ cup very cold water
   egg white for glaze (optional)

To prepare the pastry by hand, sift the sugar and flour. Using a pastry cutter or two knives, cut the butter into the flour until the mixture resembles coarse cornmeal. Beat the eggs and add them to the butter and flour mixture, stirring to combine thoroughly. The mixture should be somewhat crumbly. Add enough of the cold water to bind the dough and allow it to be formed into a ball. Take the ball of dough and put it on a lightly floured surface. Quickly knead the dough with a few swift strokes using the heel of the hand in order to assure that all of the ingredients are combined smoothly. Do not knead too much, or the pastry will be tough. Allow the pastry to rest in the refrigerator for two hours before forming.

To prepare the pastry using a food processor, combine the dry ingredients, adding the butter by tablespoonfuls on the pulse mode. Add the eggs and water, using the pulse mode until the mixture gathers into a ball. Form by hand into a ball. Wrap and chill 1 hour before using.

Yield: 30 ounces, makes enough for two 10-inch tart shells

The Cascade Dining Room, with its hand-wrought natural beauty, romantic ambiance, and celebrated cuisine, delights hotel guests from around the world and is the destination point for many Northwest travelers. In any season, the view from the dining room is spectacular. During summer, diners enjoy a vista of distant mountains from Timberline's 6,000 foot elevation. In winter, snow embraces the landscape and drifts as high as the second story dining room windows.

Hollandaise Sauce

4 egg yolks
¼ cup dry white wine
   juice of 1 lemon
1 teaspoon salt
   pinch of white pepper
   pinch of cayenne pepper
3 cups clarified butter

Note: Assemble all the ingredients and read the following instructions carefully before beginning. The preparation of this sauce requires concentration and speed.

   Combine the white wine, lemon juice, salt, and peppers in a saucepan, bring to a boil, and reduce over a very high heat until half of the liquid has evaporated. Remove the saucepan from the heat and let it cool for a few minutes.
   Add the egg yolks one at a time, beating constantly with a wire whisk. Put the saucepan back on very low heat (or over a pan of very hot water double boiler fashion). Heat the sauce again, beating it constantly. When it has become creamy, remove it again from the heat and let it cool while continuing to beat it gently.
   When the sauce is just barely cool enough to touch, begin adding the clarified butter very gradually. The first addition should be just a few drops. Beat the mixture well after each addition and add a larger quantity with each successive addition. (The added butter should be at the same temperature as the egg yolk mixture.) It is very important to fully incorporate each addition of butter before adding more.
   When the butter is fully combined, strain the mixture through a fine sieve. Serve warm.

Yield: 3½ cups

Beef Stock

4 pounds beef and/or veal knuckle bones and trimmings
2 tablespoons vegetable oil
1 onion, chopped
1 carrot, chopped
1 leek, chopped
2 stalks celery, chopped
1⅛ cups tomato paste
1¼ cups Pinot Noir (or other dry red wine)
4 quarts water
2 bay leaves
6 whole allspice berries
3 sprigs parsley
   pinch (or sprig) of thyme
8 whole peppercorns

Preheat the oven to 375°.
Place the oil and the bones in a roasting pan and brown in the oven. Turn bones occasionally to brown evenly. When lightly browned, add vegetables and tomato paste. Return to the oven and continue to brown, stirring occasionally, for 30 minutes. Add the Pinot Noir and deglaze.

Place the roasted vegetables and bones into a stock pot and add the water and seasonings. Bring to a boil, without stirring. Reduce the heat. Cook over a very low heat for 2 to 3 hours, without stirring. As the foam accumulates on the top of the stock, skim it off with a spoon. Strain the stock through a fine sieve. Chill. To remove the fat, wait until the stock is cold. Lift off and discard the solidified fat. (The stock will keep longer if the fat cap is allowed to remain in place until use.)

Yield: 8 cups

A good stock takes time, but it's the wisest investment a cook can make. An essential ingredient in soups and sauces made at the Lodge is a **mirepoix**. *This recognized flavoring made from diced carrots, onion, celery, and herbs is used to enrich and enhance a stock. At the cook's discretion, additional root vegetables such as fennel, leek, or turnip can also be added.*

Béchamel Sauce

  4 tablespoons butter
  ⅛ medium onion, minced
  3 tablespoons flour
  ½ cup milk
  ¼ teaspoon salt
  3 whole peppercorns
  1 sprig parsley
    pinch of nutmeg
  1 whole clove

In a saucepan sauté the onion in the butter until the onion is translucent. Stir in the flour. Cook a few minutes, or until it becomes bubbly and foamy. Gradually add the milk, whisking slowly. Bring to a boil, add the seasonings, and let simmer for 30 minutes, stirring occasionally to prevent burning. Strain the sauce through a fine sieve and use.

Yield: 1½ cups

Madeira Sauce or Brown Sauce

  3 quarts Beef Stock (see Master Recipe)
  ½ cup Madeira (for Brown Sauce use ½ cup dry red wine)
  2 teaspoons Kitchen Bouquet
  2 tablespoons cornstarch
  2 tablespoons water
    salt and pepper to taste

In a saucepan, simmer the Beef Stock until it is reduced to 1 quart. Simmer the Madeira or red wine in a separate pan until it is reduced to ¼ cup. Combine the reduced wine and the reduced stock. Add the Kitchen Bouquet to darken. Thicken with the cornstarch mixed with water. Simmer 5 minutes and season to taste.

Yield: 4 cups

Chicken Stock

1 pound (approximate) chicken carcasses
  (do not use chicken livers)
2 quarts water
½ onion, chopped
½ stalk celery, chopped
½ carrot, chopped
2 sprigs parsley
1 bay leaf
2 allspice berries
2 whole cloves
4 whole peppercorns
  pinch (or sprig) of thyme

The most important piece of equipment for successful cooking is your stove. Like all fine restaurants, the Cascade Dining Room uses gas stoves. Gas is the most flexible heat source, making it possible to rapidly change the temperature from a slow simmer to a rolling boil.

Wash the chicken parts (or carcasses) in cold water. Place in a stock pot with the water and the remaining ingredients. Bring to a boil. Reduce the heat and simmer without stirring 1½ hours. Skim the foam from the surface as it accumulates. Strain through a fine sieve and chill. To remove the fat, wait until the stock is cold. Lift the solidified fat from the surface and discard. (The stock will keep longer if the fat is allowed to remain in place until use.) For a richer stock, reduce further by simmering.

Yield: 4 cups

Crème Anglaise

3 cups milk
¾ cup sugar
8 egg yolks
1 tablespoon cornstarch
1 tablespoon vanilla extract

Combine the milk and sugar in a saucepan over medium heat. Stir until the sugar dissolves. Increase heat and bring to a boil. Remove immediately and set aside.

Combine the egg yolks and cornstarch in a bowl and whisk together until well blended. Add a few tablespoons of the hot milk mixture to the eggs, whisking well. Then add the egg mixture to the hot milk, whisking constantly. Cook over medium heat, whisking constantly for one minute. Do not allow the sauce to boil. Remove from the heat and add the vanilla. Let the mixture cool to room temperature, then refrigerate until thoroughly chilled.

Yield: 4½ cups

Ganache

1 pound bittersweet dark chocolate, finely chopped (use highest quality)
2 cups heavy cream

Place the chopped chocolate in a large mixing bowl. Bring the cream almost to a boil and pour it over the chocolate. Let sit for 2 to 3 minutes, then stir gently with a spoon to blend.

Yield: 3½ cups

Note: When used as a glaze, Ganache should be between 85° and 90°. If allowed to get too hot, it will lose its shine and be dull in appearance.

Raspberry Sauce

2 cups raspberries, fresh or frozen
simple syrup:
   3 tablespoons sugar
   2 tablespoons water
lemon juice

Purée the raspberries in a blender or food processor. Push the purée through a fine sieve using a rubber spatula to remove all the seeds. Bring the sugar and water to a boil in a small saucepan to make the simple syrup. Add the simple syrup to the strained purée and blend together. Add the lemon juice to taste.

Yield: 1 cup approximately

We invite you to visit the Cascade Dining Room at Timberline Lodge to enjoy the seasonal dishes featured in this book, as well as the many other regional specialties created in our kitchen.

120

Credits

The photographs illustrating Timberline Lodge recipes throughout this book were taken by Edward Gowans.

2
photo by Edward Gowans
Pinot Noir Poached Pears

6 & 7
photo by Ron Cronin

10
photo by Molly Kohnstamm

12
photo by Ron Cronin

13
photo by Edward Gowans

14
photo by Charlie Borland

15
platter by Terry Hutchinson
courtesy of Real Mother Goose
ram's head table, Cascade Dining
Room courtesy of Timberline Lodge

16
photo by Charlie Borland

17
plate by Faith Rahill
courtesy of Real Mother Goose
blueprints of Timberline head-
house courtesy of Friends of
Timberline archives

A colorful garden brightens the 50-year-old homestead of photographer Edward Gowans. A year-round gardener, Ed enjoys tending the kitchen orchard, perennial border, and honey bees. His expert eye and knowledge of food are reflected in the photography for the recipes in this book.

18
bowl by Molly Blanding
courtesy of the artist
plate by Sandra Johnstone
courtesy of Lawrence Galleries

19
photo by Kristin Finnegan

20
photo by Frank Menard

21
plate by Linda Mau
courtesy of Contemporary Crafts
Gallery
floor loom in Rachael Griffin
Historic Exhibition Center
courtesy of Friends of Timberline

22
photo by Bryan Peterson

23
bowl by Sandy Thatcher
courtesy of the artist
plater by Alyce Flitcraft
courtesy of the artist

24
plate by Ginny Conrow
courtesy of Lawrence Galleries

25
photo by Charlie Borland

26
tureen by Anne Hirondelle
courtesy of Lawrence Galleries

27
photo by Kristin Finnegan

28
photo by Charlie Borland

62
plate by Glen Burris
courtesy of Real Mother Goose

63
photo by Kristin Finnegan

64
photo by Kristin Finnegan

65
plate by Stephen Gerould
courtesy of the artist

66
photo by Ron Cronin

67
photo by Ron Cronin

68
photo by Edward Gowans

69
1937 calendar courtesy of
Friends of Timberline archives

70
plate by Don Hoskisson
courtesy of Lawrence Galleries

71
photo by Kent Powloski

72
photo by Bryan Peterson

73
plate by Christi Norman
courtesy of Northwest Crafts Center

74
photo by Ron Cronin

75
plate by Maria Simon
courtesy of the artist
Indian head illustration courtesy of
US Forest Service

76
photo by Bryan Peterson

77
bowl by Linda Taylor
courtesy of Contemporary Crafts
Gallery

78
plate by Peter Eulau
courtesy of Contemporary Crafts
Gallery
trail marker courtesy of Friends of
Timberline archives

79
photo by Edward Gowans

80
photo by Ron Cronin

81
plate by Molly Blanding
courtesy of the artist
rawhide and iron chair, Timberline
Lodge

82
platter by Charles Gluskoter
courtesy of the artist

83
photo by Bryan Peterson

84
photo by Kristin Finnegan

85
bowls by Gideon Hughes
courtesy of Real Mother Goose
platter by Don Sprague
courtesy of Contemporary Crafts
Gallery

86
photo by Kristin Finnegan

87
plate by Molly Blanding
courtesy of the artist

88
photo by Bryan Peterson

89
photo by Bryan Peterson

90
plate by Molly Blanding
courtesy of the artist
Blue Gentian Room in Rachael
Griffin Historic Exhibition Center,
Timberline Lodge

91
photo by Kristin Finnegan

92
photo by Kristin Finnegan

93
bowls by Frank Boyden
courtesy of Contemporary Crafts
Gallery
platter by Frank Boyden
courtesy of the artist

94
plate by Craig Martell
courtesy of Real Mother Goose
snow shoes courtesy of Friends of
Timberline

95
photo by Molly Kohnstamm

96
plate by Ron Fenter
courtesy of the artist
pinch pot by Alana Lea Smith
courtesy of Edward Gowans

97
photo by Charlie Borland

98
photo by Edward Gowans

99
plate by Roberta Lampert

courtesy of the artist
appliqué banner courtesy of
Friends of Timberline archives

100
bowl by Jim Craft
courtesy of Lawrence Galleries
Ram's Head Bar stool & Blue Ox
Bar table courtesy Timberline Lodge

101
photo by Wayne Aldridge

102
photo by Kristin Finnegan

103
bowl and plate by Charles Piatt
courtesy of the artist
toboggan courtesy of Friends of
Timberline archives

104
photo by Ron Cronin

105
basket by Natalie Lelora
courtesy of the artist
Trillium guest room hand-hooked
rug courtesy of Friends of
Timberline archives

106
photo by Ron Cronin

107
WPA brass platter courtesy of
Friends of Timberline archives
zig-zag log bench courtesy of US
Forest Service

108
photo by Kristin Finnegan

109
bowl by Connie Kiener

courtesy of the artist

110
plate by Reid Ozaki
courtesy of Contemporary Crafts
Gallery
wrought iron ram's head poker
courtesy of Friends of Timberline
archives

111
photo by Charlie Borland

112
photo by Edward Gowans

113
photo by Ron Cronin

120-125, Front cover
photos by Edward Gowans

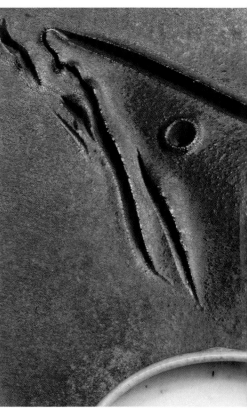

Timberline Lodge is located in the Mt. Hood National Forest and is operated by the RLK Corporation for the U.S. Forest Service.

Index